This book belongs to:

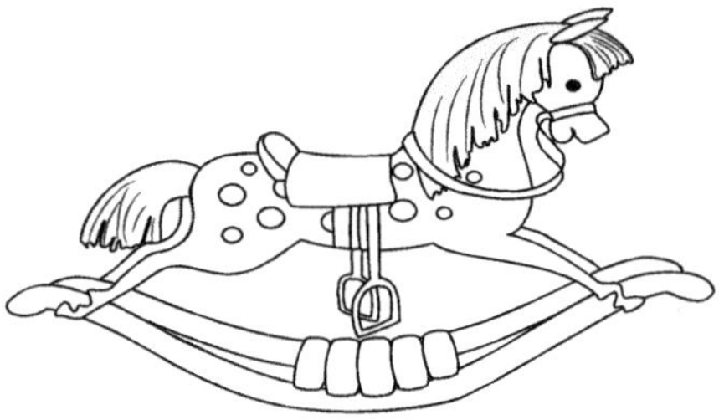

Merry Christmas!
To A Very Special Cousin
Coloring Card

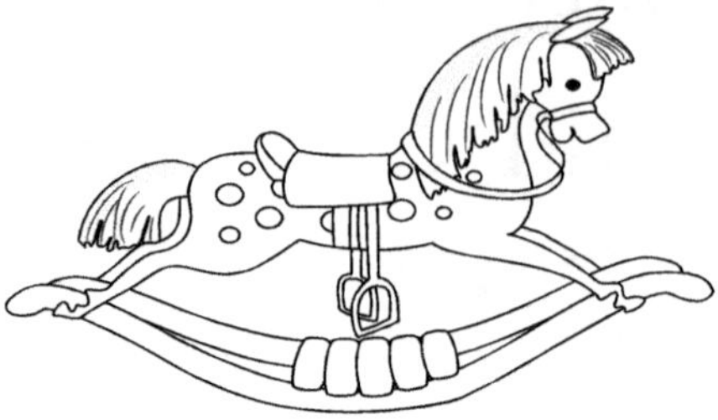

Joy to the world!

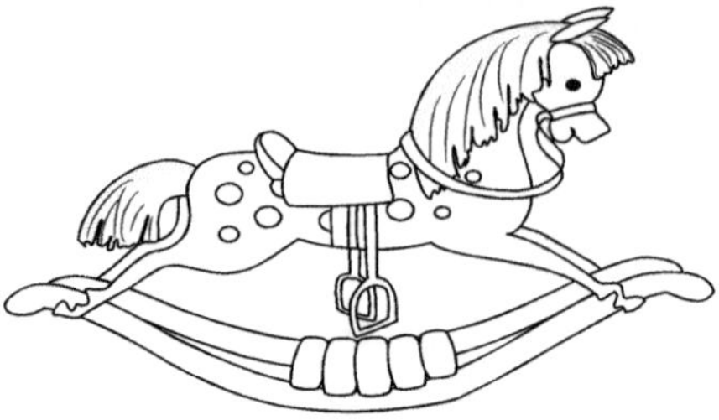

Warm wishes to you!

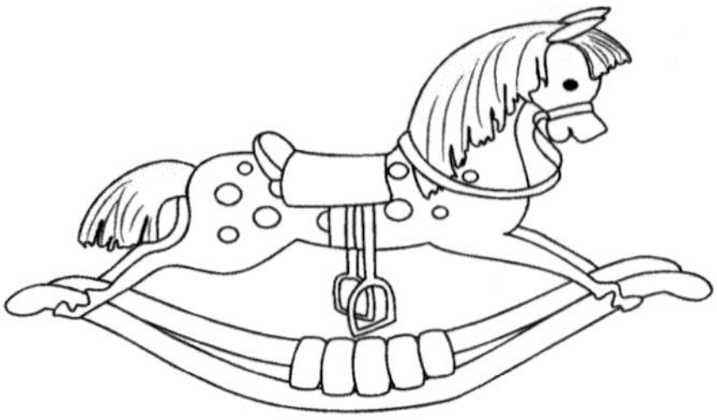

Merry and Bright!

Tis the season to be jolly,
fa la la la la la la la lamb!

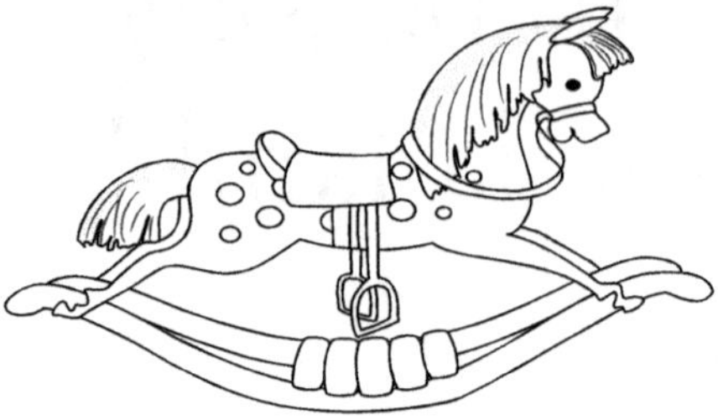

It's the best Christmas ever!

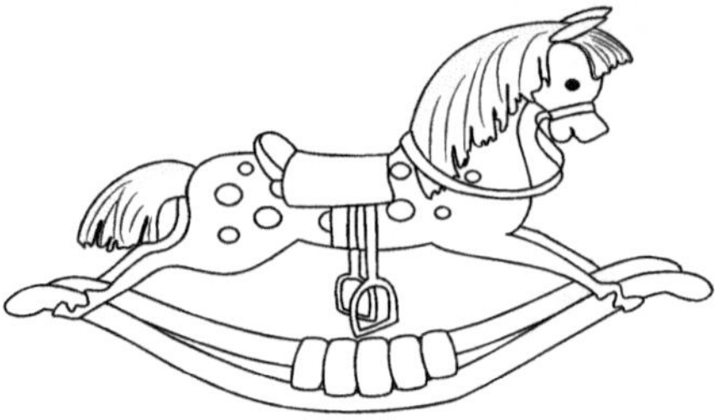

Joy to the animals!

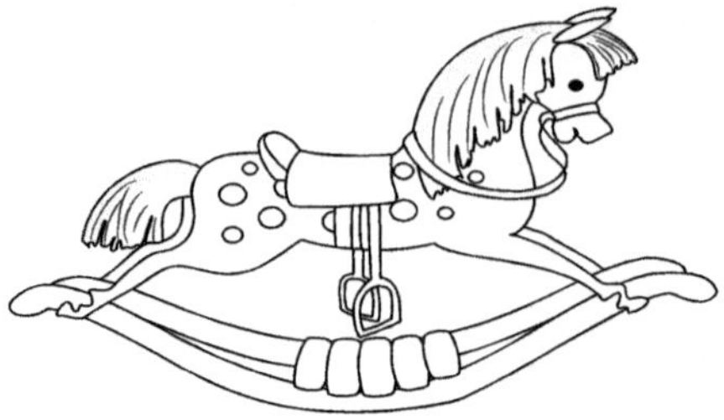

Santa's magic reindeer!

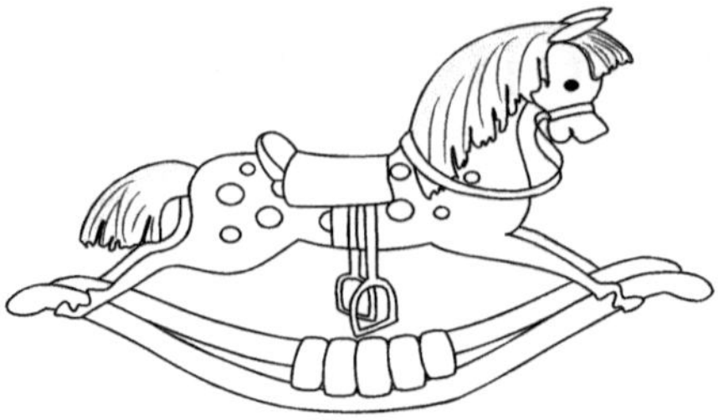

One of Santa's helpers!

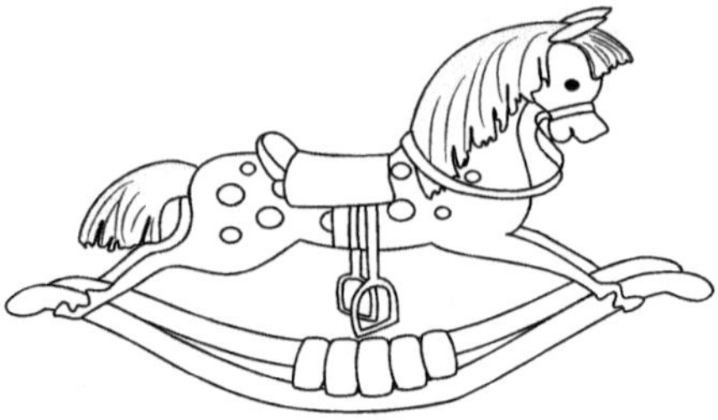

Flying in a winter wonderland!

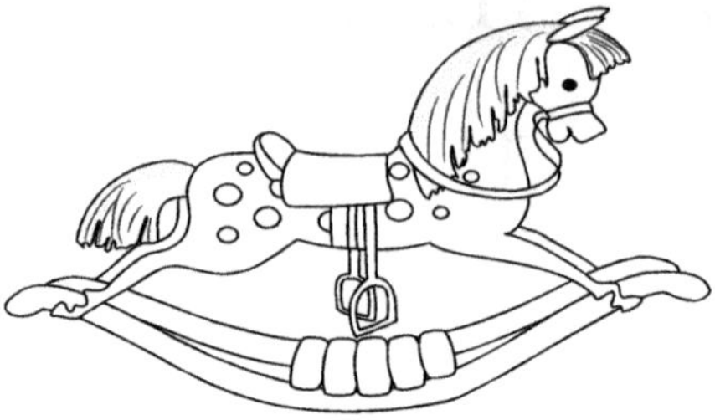

Merry Christmas

To A Very Special Cousin!

By Florabella Publishing, LLC

www.ingramcontent.com/pod-product-compliance
Lightning Source LLC
Chambersburg PA
CBHW061931270726
48660CB00003BA/1135
* 9 7 8 1 9 7 9 6 9 8 8 3 2 *